# the summer garden

a seasonal guide to making the most of your garden

# the summer garden

Richard Rosenfeld

LORENZ BOOKS

First published by Lorenz Books in 2002

© Anness Publishing Limited 2002

Lorenz Books is an imprint of Anness Publishing Limited
Hermes House, 88–89 Blackfriars Road, London SE1 8HA

Published in the USA by Lorenz Books, Anness Publishing Inc.
27 West 20th Street, New York, NY 10011

www.lorenzbooks.com

This edition distributed in Canada by General Publishing
895 Don Mills Road, 400–402 Park Centre, Toronto, Ontario M3C 1W3

A CIP catalogue record for this book is available from the British Library.

Publisher: Joanna Lorenz
Managing Editor: Judith Simons
Senior Editor: Doreen Palamartschuk
Art Manager: Clare Reynolds
Additional text: Kathy Brown, Andrew Mikolajski and Peter McHoy
Designer: WhiteLight
Photographers: Jonathan Buckley, Peter McHoy, Michelle Garrett, Peter
    Anderson, Simon McBride, Debbie Patterson, Sarah Cuttle, James
    Mitchell, Jacqui Hurst and Andrea Jones
Indexer: Hilary Bird
Production Controller: Joanna King

10 9 8 7 6 5 4 3 2 1

**page 1** Rounded heads of *Allium sphaerocephalon* contrast with the starry
forms of metallic blue *Eryngium*.
**page 2** Vivid crocosmias make a showy border display.
**page 3** *Helianthus annuus*.
**pages 4–5** Blue agapanthus with *Hemerocallis* (day lily) and pink alliums.

NOTES
In the directory section of this book, each plant is given a hardiness rating. The
temperature ranges are as follows:
**frost tender** – may be damaged by temperatures below 5°C (41°F);
**half-hardy** – can withstand temperatures down to 0°C (32°F);
**frost hardy** – can withstand temperatures down to -5°C (23°F);
**fully hardy** – can withstand temperatures down to -15°C (5°F).
In the United States, throughout the Sun Belt states, from Florida, across the Gulf
Coast, south Texas, southern deserts to Southern California and coastal regions,
annuals are planted in the autumn, bloom in the winter and spring, and die at the
beginning of summer.

# CONTENTS

# INTRODUCTION

The summer garden is usually the busiest and most radiant of the gardening year. Colours range from soft pale pastels to bright, flashy "hothouse" colours in many wonderful shades. If you have the right choice of first-rate plants you can keep your floral displays going right to the end of the season. Use big bold groups of your favourite flowers, make sure that you have plenty of scent, highlight contrasts between quiet, flowing shapes and more dramatic, spiky ones, and you will create stunning effects that can last all summer.

**left** *Crocosmia* 'Lucifer' produces tall, elegant sprays of rich red flowers, which last for several weeks. They stand out well, making a dramatic contrast against the leaves of the flamboyant cannas.

**above** A subtle, low-key summer planting with a beautiful rhythm of colours and shapes.

EVERYONE CAN CREATE A SUMMER GARDEN with plenty of character and style. With the vast range of plants now available, there are enough bulbs, annuals and perennials to stock even the biggest beds with bright colours and heady fragrances. Mixing these with carefully chosen shrubs, climbers and garden accessories will allow you to experiment with structure, colour and texture and produce superb visual effects.

## the right plant in the right place

If you have an empty bed or border, plan your design by deciding upon the overall effect you want to achieve. Do you want an area that is spare, shapely and contemporary, or packed with flowing colour as in a cottage garden?

Choose the style, and then list the best plants that will highlight and dramatize it. If you want a colourful summer display, try a traditional, beautifully free-flowing blend of three or four colours. If your bed or border is circular, place eye-catchingly tall and dramatic plants off-centre towards the middle and then work out to the edge, planting right around it.

If your favoured plant is small, place it near the edge or front of the area. Give each plant space to grow and fill out, even if that means leaving wide, irregular gaps between them in the first few years. The spaces can easily be filled with annuals, sown in the spring, and discarded in the autumn.

Make sure that your preferred colours stand out by placing them next to colours that do not compete. For example, a beautiful, soft gentle lilac will immediately be upstaged if it is placed next to a lipstick red. It is better to use other quiet pastels or greens, making an unobtrusive background. And with a plant that shoots up tall stems or sprays, such as the grass *Stipa gigantea*, which hits 2.5m (8ft) high, place it where it can be lit by the sun or stand out against a dark background.

## bedding schemes

Any scheme is a success if it makes you happy. Rules help (for example, stand taller plants towards the back, smaller ones to the front), but they do not have to be adhered to rigidly. Experiment with bright-coloured annuals, for example, you could design a flowerbed with small plants to make a patchwork-quilt effect.

Within flowerbeds you can combine a wide range of colours and textures. Subtle one-colour schemes can be charming. Try combining leaves that are matt and shiny green, olive green and pale green, to form a beautiful mix of tones, and leaves that are feathery, stumpy and round.

You can inject variety and surprise into almost any garden. Place a low-growing bed near a fun, helter-skelter bed, and include plants such as a 2m (6½ ft) high *Foeniculum vulgare* 'Purpureum' (bronze fennel) and 2.5m (8ft) high *Helianthus annuus* (sunflowers), with red and yellow *Tropaeolum tuberosum* 'Ken Aslet' climbing up them. Plant yellow-stemmed bamboos with green stripes, such as *Phyllostachys vivax aureocaulis*, to make a startling contrast against dark flowers. Add flashes of colour to any scheme by introducing hanging baskets and containers that give vitality and energy to the summer garden.

**above** Lilies look especially pleasing among herbaceous plants, which help to hide their stems. They pack plenty of impact into a small space.

**left** Roses scrambling over an archway are a quintessential ingredient of a summer country garden. As well as adding a delightful froth of blooms, prominently displayed against the sky, the screening effect of the archway gives an air of mystery to the garden.

# SUMMER PLANTS

Here is a gallery of the finest summer plants, with everything from the prettiest bulbs and annuals to sensational perennials, shrubs, roses and climbers. The following pages give all the key facts, including how high the plants grow, when they flower, their hardiness rating and, best of all, why you should grow them. With this knowledge, you should be able to select a variety of plants to design a beautiful and visually exciting summer garden.

**left** The strappy leaves of agapanthus look good with tall grasses. Blue *Agapanthus* 'Ben Hope' forms a wonderful large grouping in front of the masses of *Chionochloa conspicua.*

# bulbs

There are some splendid bulbs, corms and tubers for the summer garden. Most are well known, with some surprise inclusions that botanically belong in this section. The stars include richly scented, beautifully coloured lilies and gladioli. Alliums are incredibly popular, especially those called 'drumsticks', which have vertical stems and a ball of colour on top consisting of hundreds of tiny flowers. Dahlias are essential and provide magnificent flashes of colour through the second half of summer, sometimes until the end of autumn.

Summer bulbs are seldom used in large drifts, or with other bedding plants, as are spring bulbs. The majority of them are best treated like ordinary plants in herbaceous or mixed borders, or perhaps used to add foreground interest and colour in a shrub border.

## Agapanthus

Commonly known as the lily of the Nile or African blue lily, this genus contains about 10 species of eye-catching clump-forming plants with fleshy roots, and originates from southern Africa. The plants produce strap-shaped, arching leaves and rounded umbels of blue or white flowers, followed by wonderfully decorative seedheads.

**below left to right**
*Agapanthus* 'Ben Hope', *A. praecox* subsp. *maximus* 'Albus' and *Allium caeruleum*.

### A. 'Ben Hope'
The bell-shaped, rich blue agapanthus flowers make a magnificent display in any colour scheme. The plants flower best when they are overcrowded.
**Flowering height** 1.2m (4ft)
**Flowering time** Mid- to late summer
**Hardiness** Fully hardy

### A. praecox subsp. maximus 'Albus'
This forms bold clumps which bear large, white, trumpet-shaped flowers. It is best to grow agapanthus in a sunny border beneath a sunny wall or in pots in a soil-based compost (potting mix), and bring into a dry, frost-free shed in winter.
**Flowering height** 60–90cm (2–3ft)
**Flowering time** Mid- to late summer
**Hardiness** Fully hardy

## Allium

This is a large genus of about 700 species of perennial spring-, summer- and autumn-flowering bulbs and rhizomes, from dry and mountainous areas of the northern hemisphere. The genus includes onions, garlic and chives, and the decorative varieties are often known as ornamental onions. They produce short to tall umbels of mauve, pink, blue, white or yellow flowers, usually followed by attractive seedheads.

## A. caeruleum

The attractive umbels, composed of 30 to 50 bright blue, star-shaped flowers, sway on slender stems.
**Flowering height** 20–80cm (8–32in)
**Flowering time** Early summer
**Hardiness** Frost hardy, so provide a mulch in winter

## A. cristophii

One of the best alliums, with lilac-purple flowers, which have a rich, metallic sheen in sunlight. It is perfect for planting beneath a laburnum arch.
**Flowering height** 60cm (2ft)
**Flowering time** Early summer
**Hardiness** Frost hardy, so provide a mulch in winter

## A. hollandicum 'Purple Sensation'

A beautiful allium with umbels consisting of about 50 star-shaped, rich purple flowers. It is perfect for planting beneath a wisteria arch with tall Dutch irises.
**Flowering height** 90cm (3ft)
**Flowering time** Early summer
**Hardiness** Fully hardy

## A. karataviense

This allium originates in Central Asia. The rounded umbels consist of 50 or more small, star-shaped, pale pink flowers with purple midribs, borne on stiff stems.

The broad, grey, elliptical, almost horizontal leaves are a special feature of the cultivar.
**Flowering height** 20cm (8in)
**Flowering time** Late spring to early summer
**Hardiness** Fully hardy

## A. schubertii

The rounded umbels, which are borne on stiff stems, have inner and outer zones of small, star-shaped, mauve-blue flowers.
**Flowering height** 40cm (16in)
**Flowering time** Early summer
**Hardiness** Fully hardy

**above left to right** *Allium cristophii, A. karataviense* and *A. schubertii.*

**below** *Allium hollandicum* 'Purple Sensation' with *Lavandula stoechas.*

## Begonia

The genus was named in honour of Michel Bégon (1638–1710), a French botanist and Governor of French Canada. It contains about 900 species, some of which are tuberous-rooted. The tuberous begonias, whose tubers are dormant in winter, include the Tuberhybrida, Multiflora and Pendula types, which derive from species growing in the Andes.

### B. 'Double Orange'

This upright begonia has double orange flowers which are up to 10cm (4in) across, and look wonderful in mixed summer bedding schemes. There are also double yellow, pink, red and white begonias in varying shades.
**Flowering height** 20cm (8in)
**Flowering time** Summer
**Hardiness** Frost tender

### B. 'Giant Flowered Pendula Yellow'

The large double and single yellow flowers are 5cm (2in) across. This pendulous begonia is ideal for hanging baskets. There is also an attractive 'Giant Flowered Pendula Orange' as well as pink, white and red varieties.
**Flowering height** Trails to 20cm (8in)
**Flowering time** Summer
**Hardiness** Frost tender

### Canna 'Roi Humbert'

Commonly known as the Indian shot plant, the genus has 50 species of rhizomatous herbaceous perennials from moist open areas of forest in Asia and the tropical parts of North and South America. The genus name comes from the Greek *kanna*, "reed". Formerly known as *C.* 'King Humbert', this canna bears large racemes, 20–30cm (8–12in) long, of orange-scarlet flowers. They show up well against the striking reddish bronze, paddle-shaped leaves. The colour associates well with other bronze foliage plants such as grasses or *Foeniculum vulgare* 'Purpureum' (bronze fennel).
**Flowering height** 2.1m (7ft)
**Flowering time** Mid- to late summer
**Hardiness** Half-hardy

### Cardiocrinum giganteum

The racemes bear up to 20 fragrant, trumpet-shaped, cream flowers, streaked with purplish red inside, which grow up to 15cm (6in) long, followed by decorative seedheads. A superb plant, it needs plenty of deep, rich soil where it will not dry out in summer. It dies after flowering, but new young bulblets will mature after about four years.
**Flowering height** 2m (6½ ft)
**Flowering time** Mid- to late summer
**Hardiness** Fully hardy

### Crocosmia 'Lucifer'

The upward-facing, bright red flowers, 5cm (2in) long, are borne on tall, strong, slightly arching stems. This is an essential plant in any garden, and it is best grown in big, bold groups for maximum effect.
**Flowering height** 90cm (3ft)
**Flowering time** Late summer
**Hardiness** Frost hardy, so provide a mulch in winter

## Dahlia

The dahlia is one of the showiest flowers in the summer border. It includes about 30 species and some 2,000 cultivars of bushy, tuberous-rooted perennials from mountainous areas of Mexico and Central America. Dahlias are available in many colours, including both strident and pastel shades of yellow, orange, red, deep purple and pink as well as white. They vary in flower size from about 5cm (2in) across, as with the Pompon dahlias, to enormous flowers, almost 30cm (12in) across. They are also available as dwarf patio cultivars and large exhibition dahlias. Nearly all the medium to tall plants will need staking. Dahlia corms are planted out in early summer, dug up, and then kept dryish over winter in a frost-free place.

### D. 'Bishop of Llandaff'
A superb dahlia with bright red flowers and contrasting dark foliage.
**Flowering height** 90cm (3ft)
**Flowering time** Summer to autumn
**Hardiness** Half-hardy

### D. 'Brilliant Eye'
This is a Pompon flowerhead type. The bright red, rolled petals make neat flowers, which are only 5cm (2in) in diameter. It looks lovely with blue caryopteris.
**Flowering height** 90cm (3ft)
**Flowering time** Summer to autumn
**Hardiness** Fully hardy

### D. 'Purple Gem'
A Cactus flowerhead type with long, narrow, pointed, recurved petals that are rich purple. It is good in borders and ideal for cutting.
**Flowering height** 90cm (3ft)
**Flowering time** Summer to autumn
**Hardiness** Half-hardy

**left top to bottom** Dahlia 'Purple Gem', D. 'Brilliant Eye' and D. 'Bishop of Llandaff'.

## Eucomis autumnalis 'White Dwarf'

The small, pale green or white flowers are star-shaped and carried on a dense spike. The flower spike is topped with the familiar crown of bracts.
**Flowering height** 20–30cm (8–12in)
**Flowering time** Late summer to autumn
**Hardiness** Fully hardy

## Freesia 'Wintergold'

The fragrant, funnel-shaped flowers are yellow. Use outdoors as a summer bedding plant.
**Flowering height** 25cm (10in)
**Flowering time** Corms planted in pots in early spring will flower in midsummer. Those planted out in borders from mid- to late spring will flower in late summer.
**Hardiness** Half-hardy

## Gladiolus

The genus name is derived from the Latin word gladius, "sword", a reference to the shape of the leaves. This is a genus of about 180 species of corms with more than 10,000 hybrids and cultivars. The species are found principally in South Africa, but they also occur in Mediterranean countries, north-western and eastern Africa, Madagascar and western Asia. Apply tomato feed over the summer.

## G. 'Charming Beauty'

This hybrid has rose-coloured, funnel-shaped flowers, up to 5cm (2in) across, which are blotched with creamy white. They are borne in succession on slender flower spikes, starting at the bottom. It can survive relatively mild winters in a border, if well mulched to protect the roots from the cold.
**Flowering height** 60cm (2ft)
**Flowering time** Summer
**Hardiness** Half-hardy

## G. 'Seraphin'

The pretty, pink, ruffled flowers, up to 5cm (2in) across, each have a white throat and are borne in succession on tall flower spikes. It should be grown in a border and looks lovely near lime-green foliage.
**Flowering height** 70cm (28in)
**Flowering time** Summer
**Hardiness** Half-hardy

**above left to right**
*Gladiolus* 'Charming Beauty', *Freesia* 'Wintergold' and *Gladiolus* 'Seraphin'.

**below** *Eucomis autumnalis* 'White Dwarf'.

**above** *Lilium lancifolium* 'Tiger Lily'.

**below left to right** *Lilium candidum, L. 'Enchantment', L. regale* and *L. martagon.*

## Lilium

The genus name Lilium is an old Latin name, akin to leirion, which was used by Theophrastus to refer to *Lilium candidum* (Madonna lily), one of the oldest established plants in gardens. There are more than 100 species of bulbs in the genus, which come mainly from scrub and wooded areas of Europe, Asia and North America. They have given rise to scores of excellent hybrids, many with wonderful scents, and there are lilies for sun, shade, acid or alkaline soils.

### L. candidum

The Madonna lily has 5 or more white, faintly scented, trumpet-shaped flowers, 5–7.5cm (2–3in) long, with bright yellow anthers. They have a sweet scent and are the only lilies to produce over-wintering basal leaves. They require neutral to alkaline soil.
**Flowering height** 90cm (3ft)
**Flowering time** Summer
**Hardiness** Fully hardy

### L. 'Enchantment'

The showy, vivid orange, cup-shaped, unscented flowers, which are marked with dark purple spots, are 12cm (4³⁄₄in) across. It is excellent for the border or deep containers, where it can stay for two or three years.

**Flowering height** 60–90cm (2–3ft)
**Flowering time** Summer
**Hardiness** Fully hardy

### L. lancifolium

The confident appearance of the tiger lily is a true reflection of its fiery common name, having up to 40, but more usually 5 to 10, pinkish- or reddish-orange, purple-speckled flowers.
**Flowering height** 60–150cm (2–5ft)
**Flowering time** Late summer to early autumn
**Hardiness** Fully hardy

### L. martagon

The turkscap lily should be grown in sun or partial shade. It has glossy, nodding, unscented, pink to purplish red flowers with dark purple or maroon spots, which hang from the stems in early to midsummer. The flowers, which are 5cm (2in) across, with sharply recurring petals, were thought to resemble a Turk's cap. It is ideal growing among early summer-flowering shrubs. The naturally occurring *L. martagon* var. *album* is a desirable white form.
**Flowering height** 90–180cm (3–6ft)
**Flowering time** Early to midsummer
**Hardiness** Fully hardy

### L. regale

The regal lily, which enjoys full sun, bears large, trumpet-shaped, scented, white flowers. It can be grown in the border, although it needs support. It is excellent growing among deep red or white, late-flowering, old-fashioned roses and is suitable for large, deep pots.
**Flowering height** 60–180cm (2–6ft)
**Flowering time** Summer
**Hardiness** Fully hardy

## Sinningia

This genus embraces about 40 species of tuberous perennials and low-growing shrubs from Central and South America. The best-known is the florist's gloxinia. Position them in light or partial shade indoors.

### S. 'Etoile de Feu'

Often referred to as *Gloxinia* 'Etoile de Feu', this sinningia produces wide, trumpet-shaped, carmine-pink flowers with wavy paler margins, all summer long.

**Flowering height** 25cm (10in)
**Flowering time** Summer indoors
**Hardiness** Frost tender

### S. 'Hollywood'

Often referred to as *Gloxinia* 'Hollywood', this sinningia produces sumptuous, violet, trumpet-shaped flowers. Stand outside in a pot over summer.
**Flowering height** 25cm (10in)
**Flowering time** Summer indoors
**Hardiness** Frost tender

### Zantedeschia aethiopica 'Crowborough'

This is commonly called arum lily or calla lily and has large, white, funnel-shaped spathes, which are carried above the glossy leaves. It is found on moist soil around lakes or swamps in southern and eastern Africa.
**Flowering height** 90cm (3ft)
**Flowering time** Early to midsummer
**Hardiness** Frost hardy, so provide a mulch in winter

**above left to right**
*Sinningia* 'Etoile de Feu',
*Zantedeschia aethiopica*
'Crowborough' and
*Sinningia* 'Hollywood'.

**above** *Alcea rosea.*

**below left to right**
*Ageratum houstonianum* 'Blue Danube', *Calendula officinalis* 'Fiesta Gitana' and *Digitalis purpurea* f. *albiflora.*

# annuals

Every garden needs a lively group of annuals. They provide instant flashes of colour, are ideal for filling gaps between young plants before they flesh out, for replacing spring bedding, and for adding wherever a sudden injection of colour is needed. *Helianthus annuus* (sunflowers), from the dwarf knee-high kind to the magnificent, fast-growing giants, are one of the best when bursting out of a group of bright red perennials, for example. In the spring sow seeds in pots because out in the garden the pigeons demolish the seedlings in seconds.

### Ageratum houstonianum
Floss flowers are fluffy half-hardy annuals, mostly in shades of blue. They are ideal for edging a border and are excellent in window boxes. 'Blue Danube' forms compact hummocks of rich lavender-blue flowers, 'Blue Mink' has powder-blue flowers, 'North Star' has warm purplish-blue flowers, 'Pinky Improved' is an unusual dusky pink variety and 'Summer Snow' is a good white form.
**Flowering height** 15cm (6in)
**Flowering time** Summer
**Hardiness** Half-hardy

### Alcea
Hollyhocks are such quintessential cottage-garden plants that most gardeners are prepared to put up with their tendency to develop rust for the sake of their spires of mallow-like flowers. Plant them towards the back or middle of a border. The flowers attract plenty of butterflies. Although hollyhocks are included here with annuals, they are in fact biennials, which means that they are sown in one year to flower the next. *A. rosea* has papery-textured flowers, carried the length of tall, felted stems. Named forms include plants in Chater's Double Group, which have peony-like, double flowers in a range of colours, and the impressive 'Nigra', which has rich chocolate-maroon flowers.
**Flowering height** 2m (6½ft)
**Flowering time** Summer
**Hardiness** Fully hardy

### Calendula officinalis
The common name, pot marigold, refers to the culinary use of this hardy annual. The species has cheery, single orange flowers and aromatic, light green leaves. 'Fiesta Gitana' is a compact form, which has orange or yellow (sometimes bicoloured) flowers.
**Flowering height** 30–60cm (1–2ft)
**Flowering time** Summer
**Hardiness** Fully hardy

## Cosmos bipinnatus

With one of the longest flowering seasons of any annual, these half-hardies are of unquestioned value, quite apart from the distinction of the glistening flowers and feathery foliage. The compact plants in the Sonata Series produce carmine, pink or white, bowl-shaped flowers. 'Sonata Pink' has soft pink flowers.
**Flowering height** 90cm (3ft)
**Flowering time** Summer
**Hardiness** Half-hardy

## Dianthus barbatus

Most dianthus, commonly known as pinks, are perennials or rock garden plants, but there are also a few annuals and the appealing biennial, *D. barbatus* or sweet William, is essential in cottage gardens. Uniquely in the genus, sweet William produces flowers in dense rounded heads. The deliciously-scented flowers can be red, pink or white; some are bicoloured.
**Flowering height** 60cm (2ft)
**Flowering time** Early summer
**Hardiness** Fully hardy

## Digitalis

Foxgloves suit any cottage garden-style planting. All have spikes of characteristic, thimble-like flowers in early summer and occasionally produce lesser spikes later on. *D. purpurea* makes a good garden plant, with mounds of soft, grey-green leaves, flushed purple towards the base. It comes in shades of pink, red and purple. The pretty white form is *D. purpurea* f. *albiflora*.
**Flowering height** 1.5m (5ft)
**Flowering time** Summer
**Hardiness** Fully hardy

## Gazania

Also known as treasure flowers, most of the garden varieties are tender perennials, grown as annuals in temperate climates. They are ideal for growing along the foot of a wall. 'Daybreak Orange' has orange flowers, which stay open longer than other varieties.
**Flowering height** 20cm (8in)
**Flowering time** Summer
**Hardiness** Half-hardy

## Helianthus annuus

Sunflowers are coarse plants, but they can be splendid in isolation. 'Moonwalker' has lemon-yellow petals surrounding chocolate-brown centres. 'Music Box', a good dwarf, has a mixture of cream, yellow to dark red flowers. 'Velvet Queen' has golden-brown leaves.
**Flowering height** Up to 2.5m (8ft)
**Flowering time** Summer
**Hardiness** Fully hardy

**above** *Cosmos bipinnatus* 'Sonata Pink'.

**below left to right**
*Helianthus annuus* 'Velvet Queen', *Dianthus barbatus* and *Gazania* 'Daybreak Orange'.

**above left to right** *Lobelia erinus* 'Cambridge Blue', *Nemophila menziesii* and *Nigella damascena*.

## Impatiens walleriana

Busy Lizzies are invaluable for providing colour in shady spots. Use them at the front of borders, in containers, window boxes, and especially in hanging baskets for a long period of interest. Packed tightly, they will produce a ball of flowers. Double Carousel Mixed produces well-branched plants with double, rose-like flowers in orange, pink, red and white.

**Flowering height** 23–30cm (9–12in)
**Flowering time** Summer
**Hardiness** Frost tender

**below** *Impatiens walleriana* 'Victoria Rose'.

## Nemophila menziesii

These hardy annuals are commonly known as baby blue-eyes, because of their delightful, sky-blue, cup-shaped flowers with white centres. They should be planted near the edge of a border or in a container or window box where the flowers can be fully appreciated. In summer this carpeting species can be completely smothered in blooms.

**Flowering height** 15cm (6in)
**Flowering time** Summer
**Hardiness** Fully hardy

## Lobelia erinus

These perennial compact forms (grown as annuals) are the mainstay of park bedding schemes, while a hanging basket would be virtually unthinkable without the trailing kinds. Lobelias are among the few shade-tolerant annuals. Most are blue, although there are also selections in other colours. The compact 'Cambridge Blue', which is suitable for bedding, has mauve-blue flowers. Trailing varieties suitable for hanging baskets include those in the Cascade Series. 'Sapphire' has rich blue flowers with white eyes.

**Flowering height** 10–15cm (4–6in)
**Flowering time** Summer to autumn
**Hardiness** Fully hardy

## Nigella damascena

Love-in-a-mist is a charming, elegant annual, and is a dainty cottage-garden stalwart, almost as attractive when the seedheads develop as when it is in flower; the feathery foliage is a definite bonus. They are very easy to grow. The species is the parent of the garden strains. 'Dwarf Moody Blue' is a compact form, which can be used to make a temporary low "hedge" at the margin of a border. The flowers are sky-blue. The popular 'Miss Jekyll' has bright blue, semi-double flowers. The rarer, desirable 'Miss Jekyll Alba' is white.

**Flowering height** 20cm (8in) to 45cm (18in)
**Flowering time** Summer
**Hardiness** Fully hardy

### Oenothera biennis

Evening primrose is a stately annual or biennial, and produces a succession of flowers over the summer months that are valuable for attracting butterflies and other beneficial insects into the garden.

**Flowering height** 90cm (3ft)
**Flowering time** Summer
**Hardiness** Fully hardy

### Papaver somniferum

The opium poppy has blue-green leaves, and produces pink, purplish, red or white flowers, followed by striking seedheads. Double forms have distinctive ruffled petals. 'Hen and Chickens' has pink flowers, but is really grown for its larger than average seedheads which can be dried for winter decoration.

**Flowering height** 90cm (3ft)
**Flowering time** Summer
**Hardiness** Fully hardy

## Tagetes

Commonly known as marigolds, they are among the easiest of half-hardy annuals to grow, and provide a long-lasting display. There are two large groups, African marigolds and French marigolds. African marigolds tend to be taller and less spreading than the French.

**Flowering height** 20–45cm (8–18in)
**Flowering time** Summer
**Hardiness** Half-hardy

### T. tenuifolia

These half-hardy marigolds are bushy and produce domes of flowers. Plants of the Gem Series have single flowers in shades of yellow or orange, marked with darker colours. 'Golden Gem' is a selection with golden-yellow flowers.

**Flowering height** 15–23cm (6–9in)
**Flowering time** Late spring to early summer
**Hardiness** Half-hardy

## Tropaeolum

Nasturtiums are easy-to-grow, half-hardy annuals, with orange, yellow or red flowers. Some strains make large plants with trailing stems, which are useful for providing quick cover, although the large leaves tend to mask the flowers. The more compact forms are good for bedding. The young leaves and the flowers are edible. *T. majus* is a quick-growing climber which can spread to 2.5m (8ft).

**Flowering height** Up to 2.5m (8ft)
**Flowering time** Summer
**Hardiness** Half-hardy

**above** *Tropaeolum majus.*

**below left to right**
*Oenothera biennis, Papaver somniferum* and *Tagetes tenuifolia* 'Golden Gem' in the Jubilee Series.

above *Campanula latiloba* 'Percy Piper'.

below left to right
*Campanula lactiflora,*
*Alstroemeria* 'Morning Star'
and *Alchemilla mollis.*

# perennials

Choose plenty of perennials because they will never let you down. They keep coming up, year after year, need minimal maintenance, and can be used to create all kinds of mood, whether you want a soft, romantic garden or one that is flamboyantly smart and vibrant. They provide a fantastic range of colours, shapes and sizes, and include plenty of plants on most people's 'Top 10 Beauties'. The hardy geraniums, irises, euphorbias, lupins and poppies all bring the garden alive. They smother summer weeds, and can easily be divided in the spring if you need extra plants to give a display even more impact

## Alchemilla mollis

Lady's mantle is an essential garden plant. It is an excellent filler for gaps in borders and the frothy, lime-green, scented flowers, also good for cutting, blend with almost everything else. It makes good ground cover but can self-seed invasively. To prevent this from happening, cut off the flowers as they fade (which will also encourage further flowers).
**Flowering height** 50cm (20in)
**Flowering time** Summer
**Hardiness** Fully hardy

## Alstroemeria

Peruvian lily, or lily of the Incas, is an exquisite plant, long associated with cottage gardens. Excellent in a warm, sunny border, in cold areas they need the shelter of a wall. Leave them undisturbed after planting; they may take some years to establish. *A.* 'Morning Star' is a hybrid with rich purplish-pink flowers fading to yellow and flecked with brown from midsummer to autumn.
**Flowering height** 45cm (18in)
**Flowering time** Summer
**Hardiness** Frost hardy, so provide a mulch in winter

## Campanula

Bellflowers are stalwarts of the summer border and combine easily with a huge range of plants, especially roses. Tough and easy to grow, their refreshing blue tones are a valuable addition to almost any scheme. *C. lactiflora* is commonly known as the milky bellflower. There are a number of desirable forms of this Caucasian species, all flowering in summer. The tall, sturdy stems make them excellent for giving height to a border. 'Prichard's Variety' has violet-blue flowers.
**Flowering height** 1.2m (4ft)
**Flowering time** Summer
**Hardiness** Fully hardy

## Chrysanthemum

There are scores of showy chrysanthemums for the garden, providing a wide range of marvellous colours. They excel in the second half of summer, and in early autumn. That is when they really give the garden a lift. You can grow chrysanthemums for exhibitions with enormous blooms, but that requires all kinds of specialist techniques. For most gardeners, chrysanthemums are far better out in the garden than on greenhouse benches, where they provide fulsome sprays of mauve, red, white, yellow and orange, in flowers that range from large balls, to open stars like large daisies, to spidery shapes with thin dangly petals. Every garden should have one. Patio gardens, cottage gardens, architectural displays, and even modern gardens with all kinds of geometric shapes benefit from the late-season boost of colour and warmth that chrysanthemums provide.

### C. hybrids

The following is just a small selection, and all are hardy unless otherwise stated. 'Bronze Elegance' has light bronze, pompon flowers. 'Curtain Call' has anemone-centred, orange flowers. 'George Griffiths' is an early-flowering half-hardy form, with large, deep red, fully reflexed flowers; it is often grown for exhibition. 'Glamour' has warm, reddish-pink pompon flowers. 'Mei-kyo' is an early-flowering plant with pink pompon flowers. 'Pennine Oriel', an early-flowering plant, has anemone-centred, white flowers. 'Primrose

Allouise' is an early-flowering half-hardy sport of 'White Allouise', with weather-resistant, incurving, soft yellow flowers. 'Southway Swan' has single flowers, with silvery pink petals surrounding yellow-green centres. 'Taffy' has rich bronze-orange flowers.

**Flowering height** Up to 2m (6½ ft)
**Flowering time** Summer to autumn
**Hardiness** Mostly fully hardy

## Delphinium

These magnificent, stately plants grow in a range of colours that few other perennials can match: primrose-yellow, cream, white, pale and dark blue, mauve, pink and deep purple. A traditional herbaceous border would be unthinkable without them. There are many excellent garden hybrids, but only a few can be described here. Elatum Group plants have almost flat flowers in dense, upright spikes; Belladonna Group plants have branched stems and loose sprays of flowers. 'Blue Nile' (Elatum) is a classic pale blue delphinium. 'Casablanca' (Belladonna), which has pure white flowers with yellow centres, is an excellent choice for a pale planting. 'Clifford Sky' (Elatum) has Wedgwood-blue flowers. 'Finsteraarhorn' (Elatum) has cobalt-blue flowers touched with purple. 'Mighty Atom' (Elatum) has solidly packed spikes of semi-double, lavender-blue flowers with brown eyes.

**Flowering height** 1.2–1.5m (4–5ft)
**Flowering time** Summer
**Hardiness** Mostly fully hardy

**above left to right**
A double-flowered, reflexed florist's spray chrysanthemum, C. 'Southway Swan' and C. 'Primrose Allouise'.

**below** *Delphinium* 'Clifford Sky'.

## Dianthus

Commonly known as carnations or pinks, these bright, highly attractive plants give an exquisite touch, whether they are grown in special containers, for example old kitchen sinks or Victorian chimney pots, or right at the front of a border. The more you deadhead them, removing the faded flowers, the more they keep on flowering. Group together various different colours, and make sure that you grow some of the highly scented kind, for example the old-fashioned white, 'Mrs Sinkins'. All need wall-to-wall sun and free-draining soil. Avoid clay.

All the following are hardy. 'Bovey Belle' has double purple flowers. 'Brympton Red' has fragrant, crimson flowers with darker marbling. The scented flowers of 'Dad's Favourite' are white laced with maroon, with dark centres. 'Dawlish Joy' has variegated pink flowers. 'Doris', a bicolour, has pale pink flowers with maroon centres. 'Excelsior' has large-petalled, pink flowers; the flowers of 'Freckles' are salmon-pink, delicately blotched with red. 'Gran's Favourite' has clove-scented, white flowers laced with maroon. 'Joy' has salmon-pink flowers. 'Louise's Choice' has crimson-laced pink flowers. The miniature 'Mendlesham Maid' has white flowers with frilly petal edges. The bicolour 'Monica Wyatt' has phlox-pink flowers with ruby centres; 'Mrs Sinkins' is fragrant, with double, white, fringed flowers; 'Riccardo' is a border carnation with red and white flowers; 'White Ladies' has clove-scented, double, white flowers, purer in colour than 'Mrs Sinkins'.
**Flowering height** 45cm (18in)
**Flowering time** Summer
**Hardiness** Mostly fully hardy

## Eryngium

Sea holly is a spiky, stiffly branched, architectural plant, perhaps best given space to make its own statement, ideally in a gravel garden. It will also integrate in mixed borders, providing an excellent contrast to softer plants. Some are biennials. This striking plant has deeply cut, bluish-grey leaves, veined white, and spiky steel-blue cones of flowers.
**Flowering height** 60cm (2ft), usually
**Flowering time** Midsummer
**Hardiness** Fully hardy

## Euphorbia myrsinites

This succulent-looking species needs a degree of pampering. Grow in full sun, in a gravel garden with excellent drainage, in full sun or in troughs. The thick, almost triangular leaves are blue-green. The long-lasting, greenish-yellow flowers fade to pink.
**Flowering height** 15cm (6in)
**Flowering time** Early summer
**Hardiness** Fully hardy

## Geranium

It would be difficult to overestimate the value of these plants. Easy to grow, spreading rapidly and combining happily with a range of other plants, they are excellent in informal, cottage-garden schemes, associating particularly well with most roses. They make excellent ground cover without being invasive.

### G. 'Ann Folkard'

A fine plant, this bears a succession of magenta flowers, with blackish centres and veining, throughout summer. Early in the season the flowers are pleasingly offset by yellowish leaves, but they usually turn green by midsummer.
**Flowering height** 30cm (12in)
**Flowering time** Early summer
**Hardiness** Fully hardy

### G. 'Johnson's Blue'

A plant for every garden, this hybrid has clear blue flowers over mounds of copious green leaves.
**Flowering height** 30cm (12in)
**Flowering time** Early summer
**Hardiness** Fully hardy

### G. phaeum

The flowers, borne on elegant, wiry stems, are an unusual shade of deep, almost blackish, purple.
**Flowering height** 60cm (2ft)
**Flowering time** Early summer
**Hardiness** Fully hardy

**above** *Eryngium.*

**below left to right**
*Geranium* 'Ann Folkard', *G. phaeum, Euphorbia myrsinites* and *Geranium* 'Johnson's Blue'.

## Hemerocallis

Daylilies have trumpet-like flowers and are of great value in gardens. They make excellent border plants, rapidly forming large, vigorous clumps. Although the individual flowers last only a day (hence the common name), they are freely produced over a long period, and the grassy foliage is always appealing. Small daylilies are excellent for edging a border; the larger kinds consort happily with hostas and roses of all kinds. The species is tough enough for a wild garden.

### H. hybrids

'Jake Russell' has golden-yellow flowers with a velvety sheen in mid- to late summer. The vigorous 'Little Grapette' has deep purple flowers in midsummer. 'Lusty Leland' produces an abundance of scarlet and yellow flowers over a long period in summer. 'Prairie Blue Eyes' is semi-evergreen with lavender-purple flowers in midsummer. 'Scarlet Orbit' has bright red flowers with yellow-green throats in midsummer. 'Stafford', one of the best of its colour range, has rich scarlet flowers with yellow throats in midsummer.
**Flowering height** 60cm (2ft)
**Flowering time** Summer
**Hardiness** Fully hardy

## Iris

This large genus also includes bulbs. The plants described here are perennials. *I.* 'Blue Eyed Brunette' has distinctive rich red-brown flowers with gold beards. *I. pallida* is an excellent blue for the border. The warm lavender-blue flowers are good for cutting.
**Flowering height** 90cm (3ft)
**Flowering time** Early summer
**Hardiness** Fully hardy

## Kniphofia

Some people think of red hot pokers as vulgar, but there is no denying the impact that they can have in a garden with their luminous torch-like flowers. *K.* 'Alcazar', an archetypal poker, has bright red flowers.

**Flowering height** Up to 1.5m (5ft)
**Flowering time** Early, mid- or late summer
**Hardiness** Mostly fully hardy

## Lupinus

With their tall spires of pea flowers in a range of colours (some being bicoloured), lupins are essential for giving height to borders in early to midsummer.
**Flowering height** 90cm (3ft)
**Flowering time** Midsummer
**Hardiness** Fully hardy

## Monarda

Bergamot is an excellent border plant that bears showy heads of hooded flowers in a range of clear colours. They are ideal for a mixed or herbaceous border. 'Alba' has white flowers. *M. didyma*, or sweet bergamot, is often included in herb gardens.
**Flowering height** 90cm (3ft)
**Flowering time** Mid- to late summer
**Hardiness** Fully hardy

## Papaver orientale

Most of the perennial poppies grown in gardens are descended from this species. They are usually grouped under *P. orientale* for practical reasons; they all produce large, bowl-shaped flowers. 'Effendi' has orange-red flowers. 'Khedive' has pale pink flowers.
**Flowering height** 90cm (3ft)
**Flowering time** Early summer
**Hardiness** Fully hardy

## Pelargonium

With an endless succession of cheerful flowers, in shades of white, pink and crimson, pelargoniums are the archetypal summer plant. These (usually) evergreen tender perennials can be grown in hanging baskets, containers, window boxes or in summer bedding.
**Flowering height** Up to 45cm (18in)
**Flowering time** Summer
**Hardiness** Frost tender

**opposite from top, left to right** *Hemerocallis* 'Jake Russell', *H.* 'Little Grapette', *H.* 'Stafford', *Iris* 'Blue Eyed Brunette', *I. pallida*, *Kniphofia* 'Alcazar', Lupins, *Papaver orientale* 'Khedive' and *Monarda didyma*.

**below** *Pelargonium* 'Irene'.

**above left to right**
*Calluna vulgaris* 'Tib', *Cistus* 'Sunset' and *Buddleja alternifolia*.

**below** *Buddleja davidii* 'Nanho Blue'.

# shrubs

A good choice of shrubs will give you a strong garden structure with green leaves all year, plenty of flowers attracting butterflies and bees, and some fantastically strong scents. Most are very easy to look after, only needing trimming and shaping. If you have room, and allow them to grow, many will eventually reach the size of small trees. If you only have room for one, choose a mock orange (*Philadelphus*) for its richly perfumed white flowers.

## Buddleja

The heavily scented flowers of these medium-to-large deciduous shrubs are irresistible to butterflies. They are reliable plants for the back of a border.

### B. alternifolia

This handsome plant has pendent racemes of deliciously scented mauve flowers in early summer. Pruning easily controls its size. The form 'Argentea' is even more desirable. It has silver-grey leaves and is very effective as a standard and specimen.
**Height** 4m (13ft)
**Flowering time** Summer
**Hardiness** Fully hardy

### B. davidii

Commonly called the butterfly bush, this bears long spikes of fragrant, usually mauve flowers. It is essential in a wild or ecological garden because of its attraction for butterflies. There are several selections, all of which can be pruned hard in late winter to early spring, including 'Black Knight', which has deep reddish-purple flowers, 'Nanho Blue' with rich lavender-blue flowers, and 'Peace', which is a reliable white selection.
**Height** 3m (10ft)
**Flowering time** Mid- to late summer
**Hardiness** Fully hardy

## Calluna

This genus of heathers consists of a single species, but there are a huge number of cultivars, all evergreen and producing their spikes of bell-shaped flowers between midsummer and late autumn. Some also have coloured foliage, which provides interest over a longer period. Heathers are excellent in containers and rock gardens. *C. vulgaris* 'Tib' is the earliest double cultivar to flower, with racemes of small, double, cyclamen-purple flowers and dark green leaves.
**Height** Up to 60cm (2ft)
**Flowering time** Summer to late autumn
**Hardiness** Fully hardy

## Cistus

Often called sun rose or rock rose, in Mediterranean countries these scrubby evergreen shrubs cover large areas of open ground, as heathers do in northern Europe. The flowers, which have a papery texture, like poppies, are short-lived, but follow one another in quick succession at the height of summer. They are perfect in a gravel garden, basking in the reflected heat from the stones, and combine well with shrubby herbs. This is a good compact shrub for a small garden.

**Height** 90cm (3ft)
**Flowering time** Early to midsummer
**Hardiness** Fully hardy

## Daboecia

This genus of heathers contains two evergreen species: *D. cantabrica* and *D.* x *scotica*. They are best grown *en masse* in an open situation or in beds with other heathers or conifers. *D. cantabrica* 'Atropurpurea' has pinkish-purple flowers and bronze-tinted foliage.

**Height** 40cm (16in)
**Flowering time** Early summer to mid-autumn
**Hardiness** Fully hardy

## Fuchsia

There are thousands of hybrids of this deservedly popular genus. They flower over a long period. Some have small, dainty flowers but others are more flamboyant. Plant them in beds and borders, as wall shrubs, and in containers and hanging baskets. *F.* 'Caroline' is a half-hardy fuchsia with purplish corollas and creamy pink sepals. It is an upright plant, about 90cm (3ft) high. *F.* 'Gay Parasol' is a tender bedding fuchsia with dark red-purple corollas and sepals that are ivory, about 90cm (3ft) high. *F.* 'Royal Velvet' is a tender bedding fuchsia with large double flowers with luminous deep purple corollas and crimson sepals. It makes an exceptionally good standard and is about 75cm (30in) high.

Hardy hybrids include *F.* 'Army Nurse', with semi-double, blue-violet and deep carmine-red flowers. It makes an excellent standard. *F.* 'Hawkshead' is a popular cultivar, with single, pinkish-white flowers, which are tinged green.

**Height** Up to 90cm (3ft)
**Flowering time** Summer
**Hardiness** Fully hardy to frost tender

**above** *Daboecia cantabrica* 'Atropurpurea'.

**below left to right** *Fuchsia* 'Caroline', *F.* 'Royal Velvet' and *F.* 'Gay Parasol'.

## Hebe

These are grown for their summer flowers, which are highly attractive to bees, and for their foliage. Compact types are good in containers.

### H. 'Blue Clouds'

This excellent hybrid has long spikes of bluish-mauve flowers from early summer until well into autumn.
**Height** 90cm (3ft)
**Flowering time** Summer to autumn
**Hardiness** Fully hardy

### H. 'Great Orme'

An elegant hybrid, this has narrow green leaves and spikes of pale pink flowers, ageing to white.
**Height** 1.5m (5ft)
**Flowering time** Summer to autumn
**Hardiness** Frost hardy

## Hydrangea

They are among the few deciduous shrubs that thrive in containers. Hydrangea flowerheads take a number of forms: pretty lacecaps have a central mass of tiny fertile flowers surrounded by larger sterile flowers; mopheads (hortensias) have domed heads of sterile flowers only.

### H. arborescens

Commonly known as Sevenbark, this is less widely grown than its named selections, the loveliest of which is 'Annabelle', which produces large, cream-coloured flowerheads.
**Height** 1.5m (5ft)
**Flowering time** Late summer
**Hardiness** Fully hardy

### H. macrophylla

The stiffly growing shrub 'Altona' has flowers that are cerise-pink on alkaline soils and mid-blue on acid soils.
**Height** 1–1.5m (3–5ft)
**Flowering time** Mid- to late summer
**Hardiness** Fully hardy

## Lavandula angustifolia

Old English lavender has grey-green leaves and scented blue-grey flowers. The many selections include 'Hidcote' (syn. *L.* 'Hidcote Blue'), which has deep lavender-blue flowers; 'Munstead' which has soft, lilac-blue flowers; and the strong-growing 'Rosea' has pink flowers. All need full sun and well-drained soil.
**Height** 60cm (2ft)
**Flowering time** Early to late summer
**Hardiness** Fully hardy

## Perovskia

Russian sage produces a sheaf of whitened stems with small, mauve-blue flowers. It is excellent in a gravel or Mediterranean garden. *P.* 'Blue Spire' has silver-blue, deeply cut leaves and spires of rich blue flowers.
**Height** 90cm (3ft)
**Flowering time** Late summer
**Hardiness** Fully hardy

## Philadelphus 'Belle Etoile'

The scent of the mock orange is unmistakable and almost cloyingly sweet when it hangs in the air in early summer. Most of the plants in cultivation are hybrids of garden origin. Grow them as a fragrant backdrop to a mixed border.
**Height** 1.5m (5ft)
**Flowering time** Midsummer
**Hardiness** Fully hardy

## Potentilla

These neat, hardy, deciduous shrubs bear masses of flat, open flowers throughout the summer, in shades of red, orange, yellow, pink and white. They need sun and do well in rock gardens or at the front of borders. *P. fruticosa* is the best-known species; its many cultivars include 'Medicine Wheel Mountain', which has yellow flowers.
**Height** 90cm (3ft)
**Flowering time** Summer
**Hardiness** Fully hardy

## Rosmarinus officinalis

This aromatic shrub has dark green, narrow leaves and mauve-blue flowers in summer. 'Lady in White' has white flowers. 'Miss Jessop's Upright' (syn. 'Fastigiatus') is an upright form with light purplish-blue flowers.
**Height** 1.5m (5ft)
**Flowering time** Summer
**Hardiness** Borderline hardy

## Santolina chamaecyparis

Cotton lavender is a mound-forming shrub with finely dissected silvery leaves. It has lemon-yellow flowers in midsummer, but is principally valued as a foliage plant.
**Height** 60cm (2ft)
**Flowering time** Summer
**Hardiness** Fully hardy

**above** *Santolina chamaecyparis.*

**below left to right** *Potentilla fruticosa* 'Medicine Wheel Mountain', *Perovskia* 'Blue Spire', *Rosmarinus officinalis* and *Philadelphus* 'Belle Etoile'.

above *Rosa* 'Albertine'.

below left to right
*Rosa* 'Fragrant Cloud',
*R.* 'Elizabeth Harkness'
and *R.* 'Sexy Rexy'.

# roses

The rose is the quintessential summer flower. Many modern varieties combine a cast-iron constitution with an unrivalled length of flowering. Some are dainty and elegant, others richly coloured show-stoppers, and many are deliciously fragrant. Besides their value as climbers and ramblers, and in beds and borders, some can be used for ground cover, while those with a neat, compact habit are ideal for growing in containers.

## Rosa 'Albertine'

A vigorous rambling rose with fully double, light pink flowers, which appear in a single flush in midsummer, opening from copper-tinted buds. The rich, distinctive scent of this rose has assured its continuing popularity.
Height 5m (16ft)
Flowering time Summer
Hardiness Fully hardy

## R. 'Elizabeth Harkness'

This large-flowered rose, of upright habit, was introduced in 1969. It produces shapely, fully double, fragrant, ivory-white flowers that flush pink as they age. The leaves are semi-glossy. 'Elizabeth Harkness' is good in beds and for cut flowers.
Height 75cm (2½ft)
Flowering time Summer
Hardiness Fully hardy

## R. 'Escapade'

A cluster-flowered rose, of freely branching habit, introduced in 1967. The semi-double, sweetly scented flowers are of unique colouring: borne in clusters from summer to autumn, they are soft lilac-pink, opening flat to reveal white centres and golden stamens. The leaves are glossy bright green. A disease-resistant rose, 'Escapade' is good for cutting and in mixed plantings.
Height 1.2m (4ft)
Flowering time Summer
Hardiness Fully hardy

## R. 'Fragrant Cloud'

A large-flowered rose, of sturdy, branching habit. The fully double, richly scented, bright geranium-red flowers, ageing to purplish-red, are carried from summer to autumn. The leaves are leathery, and dark green. It is an outstanding rose that can be used in bedding and for cut flowers.
Height 75cm (2½ft)
Flowering time Summer
Hardiness Fully hardy

### R. 'Golden Showers'

This climbing rose is an enduring favourite of many gardeners. It produces clusters of double, lightly scented, yellow flowers. The flowers lack distinction, having few petals, but the reliability of this rose in a variety of situations has ensured its popularity.

**Height** 3m (10ft)
**Flowering time** Summer to autumn
**Hardiness** Fully hardy

### R. 'Ingrid Bergman'

A large-flowered rose, of upright, branching habit. The fully double, only lightly scented flowers are deep red and the leaves are glossy dark green. It is good for cutting, bedding and containers.

**Height** 75cm (2½ft)
**Flowering time** Summer to autumn
**Hardiness** Fully hardy

### R. 'Just Joey'

A large-flowered rose, of upright, branching habit. It has elegant, long, shapely buds that open to lightly scented, fully double, coppery orange-pink flowers with slightly ruffled petals. The matt dark green leaves are tinted red on emergence. 'Just Joey' is an outstanding rose, valued for its freedom of flowering, general disease-resistance and versatility in the garden, besides the unusual colour of the blooms.

**Height** 75cm (2½ft)
**Flowering time** Summer
**Hardiness** Fully hardy

### R. 'Louise Odier'

A Bourbon rose, introduced in 1851, that is suitable for training as a climber and is best with some support. From midsummer to autumn it produces clusters of cupped, fully double, strongly scented, lilac-tinted, warm pink flowers. The leaves are greyish-green.

**Height** 2.3m (7½ft)
**Flowering time** Midsummer to autumn
**Hardiness** Fully hardy

### R. 'Sexy Rexy'

A cluster-flowered rose, of upright habit, that was introduced in 1984. Clusters of shapely, fully double, lightly scented, clear light pink flowers are produced in summer and into autumn. A versatile rose, 'Sexy Rexy' is excellent for garden use, in containers, and as a cut flower.

**Height** 60cm (2ft)
**Flowering time** Summer to autumn
**Hardiness** Fully hardy

**top** *Rosa* 'Louise Odier'.

**above** *Rosa* 'Escapade'.

**below left to right** *Rosa* 'Golden Showers', *R.* 'Ingrid Bergman' and *R.* 'Just Joey'.

**above** *Bougainvillea.*

**below left to right**
*Clematis* 'Mrs Cholmondeley',
*C.* 'Royalty' and *C.* 'Bees'
Jubilee'.

# climbers

These versatile plants can be used to romp up trees, cover walls, twist round pillars and poles or cover a trellis to produce stunning masses of colour and scent.

## Bougainvillea

These evergreen climbers are grown for the brightly coloured bracts that surround their insignificant flowers. The spiny stems have to be tied to a trellis. In warm climates they are impressive over large pergolas or cascading down banks. Combining them with *Trachelospermum jasminoides* will provide the scent they lack.
**Height** Up to 12m (40ft)
**Flowering time** Summer to autumn (bracts)
**Hardiness** Half-hardy to frost tender

## Clematis

There is a superb range of summer-flowering clematis in many shades and colours. Large-flowered hybrids are excellent on walls and fences; others are good for growing through bushes, over buildings and architectural features.

## C. 'Bees' Jubilee'

A large-flowered clematis. In spring it produces masses of single, deep mauve-pink flowers, 13cm (5in) across, that lighten with age, each sepal having a darker central bar; the anthers are light brown. A second flush of smaller flowers appears in mid- to late summer.

'Bees' Jubilee', a compact and reliable clematis, is similar to the more commonly grown 'Nelly Moser'.
**Height** 2.5m (8ft)
**Flowering time** Summer
**Hardiness** Fully hardy

## C. 'Jackmanii Superba'

A large-flowered clematis that produces an abundance of velvety, rich purple flowers, 15cm (6in) across, with light brown anthers.
**Height** 3m (10ft)
**Flowering time** Mid- to late summer
**Hardiness** Fully hardy

## C. 'Mrs Cholmondeley'

It has single, pale lavender-blue flowers, to 13cm (5in) across. 'Mrs Cholmondeley' has one of the longest flowering seasons of all clematis.
**Height** 3m (10ft)
**Flowering time** Summer
**Hardiness** Fully hardy

## C. 'Royalty'

In late spring to summer this large-flowered clematis produces an abundance of semi-double, purplish-mauve flowers, 15cm (6in) across, with pale yellow anthers. Later flowers, from midsummer to autumn, are smaller and single. 'Royalty' tolerates any aspect.
**Height** 1.8m (6ft)
**Flowering time** From late spring to summer
**Hardiness** Fully hardy

### Jasminum officinale

This is a twining, highly-scented climber with small white flowers. 'Aureum' has leaves splashed with yellow.

**Height** 5m (16ft)
**Flowering time** Summer
**Hardiness** Frost hardy

### Lathyrus grandiflorus

This suckering species has glowing pinkish-purple flowers in summer and is good in a wild garden.

**Height** 2m (6½ft)
**Flowering time** Summer
**Hardiness** Frost hardy

### Lonicera periclymenum

A common woodlander in Europe, the honeysuckle has scented, creamy-white flowers in summer. There are three excellent forms. 'Belgica' has pink and red flowers, followed by red berries. 'Graham Thomas' bears copper-tinted, creamy flowers. 'Serotina' has purple and red flowers.

**Height** 3m (10ft)
**Flowering time** Mid- and late summer
**Hardiness** Fully hardy

### Passiflora caerulea

Passionflowers are highly distinctive climbers, with ten outer petals surrounding a crown of central filaments, inside which are the prominent stamens and styles. The summer flowers are white, with the filaments banded blue, white and purple. The form 'Constance Elliot' has fragrant, creamy white flowers with red stigmas.

**Height** 6m (20ft)
**Flowering time** Summer to autumn
**Hardiness** Borderline hardy

### Solanum crispum

These delightful climbers deserve to be better known. They produce an abundance of potato flowers over a long period and are generally easy to grow in well-drained soil in full sun. The best form 'Glasnevin', which can be evergreen, has deep blue flowers, with prominent central yellow 'beaks', which are carried in clusters over many weeks in summer. *Solanum jasminoides* 'Album' has lovely yellow-centred, white flowers.

**Height** 5m (16ft)
**Flowering time** Summer
**Hardiness** Borderline hardy

**above left to right**
*Jasminum officinale* 'Aureum', *Solanum crispum* 'Glasnevin' and *Lonicera periclymenum*.

**below left to right**
*Clematis* 'Jackmanii Superba', *Lathyrus grandiflorus* and *Passiflora caerulea*.

# SUMMER DISPLAYS

A summer garden in full bloom is delightful. Dominant colours come and go with perennial poppies and dahlias flinging out brightly coloured flowers and then fading away. Foxglove spires pop up among shrubs, and hardy geraniums flower in blue, pink, red and white, while old-fashioned roses unleash beautiful displays in midsummer. The key to success is making sure that you have a succession of flowering plants, always providing surprises, from early summer until autumn sets in.

**left** A lively informal border display, mixing shrubs, perennials and biennials, with lilac-blue perovskia, pink and cream hollyhocks, buddleia and purple verbena.

# scented gardens

**above left** A simple trellis arbour and wooden bench are surrounded by heavily scented plants, including a free-flowing jasmine.

**above right** A window box planted with nicotiana and heliotrope, here in a sophisticated all-white colour scheme, will bring the sweet scents of the flowers into the home.

Summer gardens need plenty of scent. Roses are always favourites, but there are many more rich, intriguing scents on offer. With the right choice you can have the fragrance of pineapple (from *Cytisus battandieri*), marzipan (*Heliotropium*), and even chocolate (*Cosmos atrosanguineus*). Mix scented plants with showy but less fragrant flowers such as crocosmia and agapanthus to create pretty displays.

## sheltered corners

When growing scented plants, you want the perfume to hang in the air. It is no use growing fragrant honeysuckles, lilies and daphnes in open or windy parts of the garden where the scent will get blown away. You need to grow them in sheltered sites in full sun, where the plants will flower well, and where you can sit and enjoy them to the full. Good sites are under windows – climbers such as roses and jasmine can even reach bedroom windows – and near doors. A must for patios where you sit outside in the evening is night-scented stock (*Matthiola bicornis*), which is easy to grow and at dusk its intoxicating perfume hangs heavy in the air.

**right** A pretty, fragrant border of *Lilium regale* (regal lily), roses and lavender.

One of the best lilies you can grow is *Lilium regale*. Plant it in the autumn, and they will come up every year bearing large, exciting, white trumpet-shaped flowers with the most amazing scent. They need to grow among other perennials, for example hardy geraniums and penstemons, which can take over once the lilies finish flowering.

Slugs are the main enemy of lilies, biting through their stems. If you cannot eradicate them in your garden grow the lilies in pots, and put horticultural gravel on the soil surface. In flowerbeds, scatter grit around the lilies, and ensure your pond has plenty of hungry frogs, which devour the slugs at night.

## extra summer scents

Most of the daphnes flower in the spring, but one that flowers sporadically through the summer is the sweetly-scented *D. tangutica*. Lilacs are big shrubs and trees, and there are some first-rate choices in the 4m 4m (13ft) high range. *Syringa pubescens* subsp. *microphylla* 'Superba' keeps flowering, in bursts, all summer. *S. x josiflexa* 'Bellicent' (pink flowers) is small enough, at 3m (10ft) high, for most gardens, and is heaven in early summer. Other scented shrubs include *Philadelphus* (mock orange), while *Nicotiana sylvestris* (tobacco plant) is a good choice of annual. *Oenothera biennis* is an excellent biennial that self-seeds round the garden. The yellow flowers release their scent in the evening.

## highly scented climbers

The top scented summer climbers include roses, honeysuckle and jasmine. One of the best roses is the beautiful bright red 'Crimson Glory, Climbing', which has pointed buds, opening to wide, velvet-like petals with a heavy, rich scent. At 5m (16ft) high, most gardens have room for one. 'Gloire de Dijon' is a buff yellow, and grows equally high, and if you want one of the darkest of the scented climbing roses, 'Guinee' (also 5m) is a striking rich crimson. Put any of these reds near the white jasmine, *Jasminum officinale*, for a marvellous show. The latter needs to twist and twine around a support, such as a drainpipe up the side of the house or an old, stout tree.

**above left** A mature honeysuckle will perfume an enclosed patio area during early summer evenings.

**above right** *Gladiolus communis byzantinus* and *Cistus purpureus* make an audacious pink colour combination in the garden. Combine with pink, scented roses to add fragrance to the border.

**left** The soft pink climbing roses give out a heady summer scent and create an interesting effect against the pastel pink and blue fence.

**right** In a small garden, make every corner earn its keep. This wooden and brick unit provides seating and can be filled with flowers and herbs.

**below** Clematis-clad, bamboo trelliswork with symmetrical patterning creates a perfect backdrop to a border.

# garden ornament

The best summer gardens are kept lively and interesting not just by the choice of plants, but by using a wide range of creative ornaments. These can be expensive and elaborate, low-key and rustic – whatever will best highlight the style of the garden and emphasize its personality. If you choose attractively shaped items, they will look good when they are offset with summer flowers, and really stand out during winter when most plants are taking a rest.

The range of objects can include everything from beautiful circular tables made of wood or stone and highly distinctive kinds of trellis, to more natural shapes like driftwood. Try painting metal poles in bright colours and fixing silver globes on top. You can even paint a dead tree that has been reduced to a few spare branches a strong colour, such as electric blue, to provide an extraordinary feature that will blend or contrast with the garden.

## theatrical props

Even surprisingly everyday ornaments can be turned into wonderful, eye-catching features. Place a good-looking bench or urn at the end of a path or vista, and it immediately becomes a focal point. Once it takes on that role, dress it up and have fun. A statue can be given extra elegance by trailing a few stems of a small-leaved ivy around it, or frame it within a semi-circle of evergreen hedge or brightly coloured shrubs. Night-time lighting makes it even more potent and dramatic when it is one of the few parts of the garden being picked up by a spotlight.

Benches can be given extra prominence by siting them in a large space, where the lawn turns to gravel or paving, and the background planting, such as a clematis or climbing rose, is trained up a rustic fence. You can create a quiet, relaxing and beautiful place in the summer garden with careful planting.

**left** A floral arbour makes a rich decorative frame for a statue. The delicate shades of pink and purple roses, clematis and foxgloves make a pretty surround.

**below** Create a relaxing seating area by surrounding a bench with raised beds packed full of summer blooms.

# containers

These are an excellent way of growing even more plants during the summer, in all kinds of surprising, unlikely places. Hanging baskets can be used beside outside doors, on sheds and pillars, and window boxes on walls at the end of the garden. Whenever you see a space on a wall, imagine it filled with containers packed with brightly coloured plants. The most sensational display is a bright white wall with 20 or 30 small pots, nailed up in rows. Plant them with pelargoniums, which come in all colours from soft salmon pink to brash red, or your favourite herbs.

**above** A hanging basket with trailing begonias in all its summer glory.

**above right** A terrace wall is ideal for pots full of bright pelargoniums.

**below** A pretty mix of purple lobelia and yellow *Bidens ferulifolia.*

## tiered planting

If you have a small space, make the best use of it by packing in plants close together. Do it imaginatively, and the pots will be totally hidden by growth.

You can use all kinds of effects to create the tiers. Arrange pots on the top of a wall (firmly fixed in place) with more beneath, or nail up metal shelves. Try creating mobile herbaceous borders using dozens of pots on three platforms, 30cm (1ft), 60cm (2ft) and 90cm (3ft)

high, supported by bricks and strong boards. With over 200 plants you can transform a display into a mini tropical jungle. It will look stunning if you include plenty of lush foliage plants, along with occasional vivid flashes of red, pink, orange, yellow and white flowers.

## foliage plants

Fun, unusual foliage plants that can be grown in pots include *Glaucium flavum* (yellow horned poppy), which has the most marvellous fleshy, blue-green, cabbage-like leaves, hairy stems, and 5cm (2in) wide yellow, poppy-like flowers that last a couple of days, followed by long seedheads.

The American *Darmera peltata* has dramatically veined, dark green leaves that grow 60cm (2ft) wide. *Ligularia stenocephala* 'The Rocket' has tall black flower stems and toothed leaves. And a rarely grown star is *Colutea* x *media*, which has blue-green foliage, and curving orange flowers, followed by translucent 8cm (3in) long pods.

# window boxes

Inject lots of colour into a window box by cramming the plants close together. As long as you keep feeding them, the stress caused by overcrowding usually prompts them to flower prolifically. Try creating a lively summer display based on one dominant colour, such as blue, including different tones and hues, drawing the eye in to explore the subtle differences.

If you want strikingly contrasting schemes, use plenty of primary colours, with red and white, and blue and yellow, and a couple of trailing plants that lead the eye away, like the yellow *Bidens ferulifolia* with its prolific show of star-shaped flowers. If you have a courtyard, fill it with window boxes at different levels, which will help add colour at all heights.

**above** Blue petunias, blue brachycome daisies and *Convulvulus sabatius* offer similar hues and a lively mix.

**left** Mix flame reds and earthy-brown by planting up a terracotta window box with red zonal pelargoniums, red and yellow nasturtiums and red verbena.

## distinctive displays

There are various ways of making sensational summer displays of pot plants. By grouping pots together you can create a big, dramatic show, with the containers largely hidden by the plants. Or use large, beautifully shaped containers, either standing alone or in small groups. Smaller, less eye-catching plants can produce wonderfully subtle effects in a group of attractive, rustically weathered pots. This kind of arrangement is particularly good for herbs.

## star plants

Evergreen hebes have strong shapes and can easily be trimmed to keep them looking neat. They have spiky flowerheads in shades of blue, mauve, pink, red and white. Often the flowers fade as they age, so that the spikes are coloured at the ends and white lower down. Even better, there are plenty of small ones for pots, such as *Hebe* x *franciscana* 'Variegata', which has flashy yellow and green leaves and purple flowers. It grows 60cm (2ft) high and wide.

The South American cannas provide large, exotic, paddle-shaped leaves, and tall spikes of flowers that look like gladioli. Most have fresh green leaves, but those of 'Durban' are striped green and pink, while 'Wyoming' has leaves with a strong tinge of purple.

If you want to be even more exotic, try *Chamaerops humilis* (the bushy palm). In southern Europe, where it grows wild, it can grow 3m (10ft) high, but cramped in a pot, only half that. It has stiff, fan-shaped leaves in bluish grey-green. Though half-hardy, it will easily survive in a sheltered city garden.

**above** This weathered stone vase is a classic form suitable for placing on the ground or on a pedestal. Planted with bright red cannas and pelargoniums, it makes a bold statement.

**right** This pot has been painted with pink stripes to match the delicate pink and white flowers of this hebe.

## top care tips

When planting your containers, make sure that you put plenty of drainage material in the base. Plastic foam chips or broken plant trays are effective and easy to come by. If the pot is light and liable to be blown over, it may be better to use heavy pebbles.

For plants that don't like dry conditions, a loam-based compost (soil mix) will dry out less quickly than the soilless types, and mixing in water-retaining gel will also help. A layer of shingle or large stones on the surface will reduce evaporation. It will also stop moss forming on the soil in wet weather, keep off slugs and snails, and set off the plants nicely.

You also need to give the plants a regular liquid feed in the summer because all the nutrients in the soil get washed out after about six weeks. Regular watering is crucial since roots cannot reach for reserves deep in the ground, and in sunny positions pots dry out extremely rapidly, so it is best to stick to drought-loving plants in these areas. If the roots curl out of the pot, either trim them back or move the plant into a larger container.

**above left** The choice of mellow terracotta pots, simply planted, set against the honey tones of the stone wall and gravel surface visually raises the temperature in this little courtyard.

**above right** Begonias will tolerate sunny conditions and make good planting companions for coleus and lampranthus.

**left** Nasturtiums associate well with tall, bold sunflowers in this large container.

# garden schemes

The Victorians created better summer bedding schemes than anyone, with elaborate, ornate patterning in flowerbeds, using a wide variety of plants. And while it looks incredibly difficult, it is not. Try it on a small scale in a spare bed.

Start by drawing a plan, and keep it simple, with straight lines and rounded curves, avoiding tight angles and intricate shapes. Big and bold is best to begin with. Stick to four or five colours and plant up the design with annuals, making sure that you choose neat, uniform varieties that will not spoil the pattern as they grow.

## free-flowing pathways

The arrangement of paths in the garden will have a big effect on the overall atmosphere – you can go for straight, clean geometric lines, or softly curving and winding ones.

**above** This watercourse is superbly laid out in a natural scheme, with an exciting range of flowers flourishing among the rocks.

**right** Different shades of *Impatiens*, busy Lizzie, are beautifully set off by silver-leaved plants in an elaborate, formal edging.

**far right** In this subtle informal scheme, arching, sword-like leaves are almost as important a feature as the bright blue agapanthus and orange crocosmia flowers.

**right** Metalwork arches clothed with pink and purple roses define a grass pathway bordered by blue veronica.

**below** A winding gravel path leads the eye down this narrow garden to a pretty octagonal summer house.

Paths can be made of decking, gravel, grass, pebbles, stone or frost-resistant bricks in a variety of patterns. Decking looks good but can be slippery in wet weather. Grass is sensational when mown on a bright day, but can get muddy in heavy rain. Gravel avoids both problems, always looks good, and can be covered with a top layer of more expensive coloured chippings or pebbles in different colours. Bricks or pavers laid in a herringbone pattern, for example, introduce a mellow warmth to the garden.

Grass paths are best among traditional cottage garden schemes, with arches of climbing roses or with fences and trailing climbers. To stop the grass growing into the beds, edge the paths with attractive terracotta 'rope' tiling.

boxes often demand that they are arranged in straight, military lines. On a much larger scale you can try something like a flamboyant metal "sunshade", doubling as an aerial sculpture. It will mix with an adjoining show of traditional summer plants, and makes an elegant, architectural feature, which mushrooms out of the ground.

## ethnic

An interesting alternative to the modern or rustic look, is adding ethnic shapes and colours. You can use authentic materials such as Moorish tiles, incorporate water features and large urns, or amalgamate your favourite ideas. Keep the design simple and use a mix of potted plants, lots of green foliage and a few flashes of bright colour. By lime-washing or painting walls white, a soft cream or completely beige, and creating a patterned pebble "patio", the whole area is transformed. You can also use small coloured tiles in raised ponds, grapes over a pergola, and rock gardens to add a touch of the Mediterranean. Make sure your choice of plants suits the style of decoration.

**above** Complex garden designs can be created using versatile modern materials. Harsh lines can be softened using plants such as foxgloves and zantedeschias.

## modern metal

Materials such as galvanized metal, zinc and stainless steel are being increasingly used in innovative, modern garden designs. They give a contemporary twist even to quite conventional planting schemes. They are ideal with modern architecture.

Raised metal beds and containers need stylish planting. Large succulents and cacti catch the eye, as do blue-grey cabbages, a range of flowering and aromatic herbs and even simple plantings of carnations (*Dianthus*). The hard square shapes of the

**right** Zinc containers are light enough for roof terraces and give a strikingly contemporary look to a garden.

**opposite** A backdrop of sunbleached shutters and a faded wall sets the Mediterranean atmosphere in this courtyard garden.

**above** A statue will always add interest, especially as a centrepiece in a pond.

**above right** Pots of busy Lizzies and pelargoniums make a vibrant surrounding for this lily pond.

**right** A gentle stream edged with rocks and subtle-coloured flowers provides a perfect setting for relaxing.

# waterside gardens

There are many ways water can be used, from Islamic-style ponds in courtyards to mock hillside streams. The latter need pumps and pipes to keep the water circulating. Gardens with pronounced slopes are often hard to plant, but mock streams add a real flourish, and can be set off with rocks, pond plants, and architectural features right at the top emphasizing the sense of height. Use tall grasses to hide where the water runs into the pipe and to create the illusion that the stream runs away underground instead of being pumped back to the start.

On hot, dry, free-draining slopes grow drought-tolerant seaside or Mediterranean-style plants that can cope with long periods without water. With rich soil and sun, there will be plenty of suitable plants such as lavender, euphorbia, broom and cistus. However, you need not aim for the greatest possible variety, as in a typical garden scheme, but rather select a few colourful plants and let them ramble and roam and spread in a totally uncontrived way. It is back-to-nature gardening.

**left** In this seaside garden, the steep border has been landscaped with rocks and summer-flowering plants.

**below** A Mediterranean-style garden filled with lavender, cistus, euphorbia and asphodels reflects the luxuriance of sunny scrublands.

## sweeping gardens

Larger rural gardens can be planted in natural ways. That means creating large swathes of plants that flower in the summer, much as they are found in the wild where they self-seed and spread unchecked. In this way, plants that may not look particularly exciting as individuals, and which are generally used as background elements, can often be as impressive as the more glamorous plants that usually get star billing.

Such a scheme can be successful with a minimum of maintenance if you match the plants to the conditions. In a damp, shady area, stick to plants that thrive in such a site. There is a surprisingly large choice.

# SUMMER TASKS

The most important thing is to enjoy the garden during the summer. For a few months everything is madly flourishing, and the best way to keep the garden looking good is to make sure you do four things. Keep weeds under control, water young plants with short roots the moment they start to flag, mow the grass but never too severely, and look out for pests in the greenhouse, attacking any with biological controls. Hungry birds should pick off pests in the garden; see if that happens before using chemical sprays.

**left** Dramatic red hot pokers, purple globe thistles and dahlias make a bold, bright display.

**right** Deadhead lilacs as soon as they have finished flowering. Cut back to the first pair of leaves below the flowerhead.

## plants at their best

- *Alchemilla mollis*
- *Allium*
- *Aquilegia*
- *Begonia*
- *Buddleja globosa*
- *Calendula*
- *Calluna vulgaris*
- *Cistus*
- *Cosmos*
- *Dianthus*
- *Digitalis*
- *Euphorbia*
- *Geranium*
- *Gladiolus*
- *Iris germanica* hybrids
- *Laburnum*
- *Lavandula*
- *Lupinus*
- *Nepeta x faassenii*
- *Paeonia*
- *Papaver orientale*
- *Philadelphus*
- *Rosa*
- *Tagetes*
- *Weigela*
- *Zantedeschia*

# early summer

This is usually a busy time of year. The weather can be very variable, ranging from sudden late frosts, when you have to run out and cover tender plants, to the hottest day for nine months, when everything in the greenhouse bakes.

Early summer is also the period when any spring-sown seedlings should be putting on good growth and will need potting up or planting out in the garden. The weeds will be thriving as well as everything else, and it is vital that they are promptly removed before they take hold. Some are quick to flower, and if they are allowed to scatter their seed the problem will become much worse. Pests and diseases are also starting to thrive, and prompt action now will stop them from getting out of control, necessitating more drastic measures later. If you have a heavy rainfall early in the season, it is a good idea to apply a thick mulch to the flowerbeds, to help conserve moisture for the drier months ahead. A mulch also acts as an excellent soil conditioner.

Ironically, despite all the tasks that need doing, early summer can often be a disappointing time in the garden. The spring plants have finished, and the summer plants are not yet in their stride. If the garden looks a bit quiet and plain, it's only temporary and everything will be flourishing within a few weeks.

**below** Thin seedlings, discarding the surplus ones, so that they do not become overcrowded.

**below** Biological pest controls can be very successful if used properly.

**above** Keep hanging baskets, tubs and patio pots well watered, and they will reward you with ever more abundant flowers throughout the summer.

## the flower garden

❖ Give a thorough weed and apply a thick mulch, if not already done
❖ Sow daisy seed outdoors
❖ Sow hardy annuals
❖ Finish hardening off and planting tender plants
❖ Arrange containers for summer display
❖ Plant succulents for summer display
❖ Plant overwintered pelargoniums in beds and containers for summer display
❖ Plant chrysanthemums and marguerites in containers for summer display. Place in a bright, sheltered position
❖ Plant sunflower seedlings for late-summer display
❖ Pinch out shoots of chrysanthemums, marguerites and *Osteospermum* to encourage bushy plants
❖ Stake herbaceous plants
❖ Deadhead bedding plants regularly to ensure new buds develop
❖ Prune *Syringa* (lilac) and spiraea
❖ Watch out for signs of mildew and aphids on roses, and spray promptly if found

**above** If vine weevil grubs destroy your plants by eating the roots, try controlling them with a parasitic eelworm, which can be watered into the soil.

## the greenhouse or conservatory

❖ Sow seed of biennial bedding plants, such as *Erysimum cheiri* (wallflowers), in seed trays for the next spring
❖ Feed pot plants regularly
❖ Take leaf cuttings of *Saintpaulia* (African violets) and *Streptocarpus*
❖ Start to feed tomatoes when the first truss of fruit has set
❖ If necessary, use biological pest control for greenhouse pests
❖ Pot up and pot on seedling pot plants as it becomes necessary
❖ Keep temperatures stable by using greenhouse shading, and increase ventilation
❖ Increase humidity by spraying water

**left** Plant up a mixed window box with trailing and foliage plants. Arrange the plants before actually planting to judge the final effect you will achieve.

**above** To layer shrubs, bend down a stem in a shallow hole, peg it and cover with soil.

**below** Take semi-ripe cuttings of shrubs 5–10cm (2–4in) long. Choose shoots that are fully grown except for the soft tip. The base should be hardening.

# midsummer

Midsummer is a time for enjoying the results of your earlier efforts. There are always jobs to be done, of course, but you should also make time to relax. As most things are sown or planted, the emphasis is on weeding, watering and feeding. In dry summers water shortages can be a problem, but when you do water, do it thoroughly, as shallow watering will encourage surface rooting and make the plants even more vulnerable to drought.

Midsummer is a great time for assessing what looks good in the garden, and what could look even better. Take photographs and make notes, and start planning right now for next year's display. This is also a good time to move plants around. Always keep the rootball intact, and move it with as much of the soil as possible. If the roots do get severed, then cut back the top growth and remove the flowers to give the plant a good chance to recover. Water them in well and they should recover fairly quickly.

## plants at their best

- Agapanthus
- Alcea
- Althaea
- Astilbe
- Begonia
- Calendula
- Cardiocrinum giganteum
- Cistus
- Clematis
- Cleome hassleriana
- Cosmos
- Digitalis
- Eryngium
- Gazania
- Geranium
- Gladiolus
- Hardy annuals
- Helianthemum
- Helianthus annuus
- Hydrangea
- Hypericum
- Jasminium officinale
- Kniphofia
- Lavandula
- Lilium
- Lonicera periclymenum
- Lupinus
- Monarda longifolia
- Nigella damascena
- Philadelphus 'Belle Etoile'
- Potentilla
- Rosa
- Summer bedding
- Verbascum
- Zantedeschia

**above** Carefully remove newly developing flower buds on your chrysanthemum plants to encourage larger flowers later in the season.

## the greenhouse or conservatory

- Feed pot plants regularly
- Take semi-ripe cuttings of shrubs
- Feed tomatoes and chrysanthemums regularly
- Remove sideshoots and yellowing leaves from tomatoes regularly
- Keep a vigilant watch for pests and diseases
- Thin out the young fruit on grape vines
- Regularly check container plants and water twice a day if necessary
- Most tender plants should be outside now, where they benefit from the fresh air
- Thoroughly clean all pots that are no longer required, and store away
- Beware of high temperatures. Use shading and ventilation as necessary
- Spray water on the floor and benches to increase the humidity

**above** Divide flag irises by trimming the stumps to 5–8cm (2–3in) long. Replant the pieces of rhizome on a slight ridge of soil, covering the roots but leaving the tops exposed.

**above** To layer carnations, make a slit in a non-flowering shoot, below the lowest leaves. Peg the shoot into the soil.

## the flower garden

- Apply a rose fertilizer once the main flush of flowering is over
- Feed greedy plants like geraniums and occasionally give a foliar feed
- Cut back lavender heads after flowering
- Deadhead bedding and border plants regularly to ensure new buds develop
- Hoe beds and borders regularly to keep down any weeds
- Divide and replant border irises
- Take semi-ripe cuttings
- Clip beech, holly, hornbeam and yew hedges towards the end of the period
- Layer shrubs and carnations
- Plant colchicums, to flower in the autumn, when they are available
- Transplant biennials and perennial seedlings to a nursery bed
- Order new bulb catalogues and bulbs for autumn delivery
- Disbud early-flowering chrysanthemums
- Mow the lawn except in very dry weather

**above** Use scissors, a sharp knife or secateurs to snip off dead flowerheads neatly and cleanly where they join the stem.

**below** Regularly pinch or cut out the sideshoots on cordon tomatoes.

**above** Plant prepared hyacinths for early flowering as soon as they are available.

# late summer

This is usually a time of hot, dry weather, when there is a natural lull in the garden, and the efforts of spring and early summer sowing will have paid dividends. The chores of early autumn can wait until the holidays are over and cooler weather begins to return. Most of this month's work in the garden involves watering and routine maintenance like mowing and hoeing, and clipping hedges.

If you are tempted to leave any tender plants outside all winter, seeing if they will survive, then take some safety precautions. Snip off a few cuttings, and pot them up, tending them all winter just in case the parent gets killed. Constant soaking wet soil is as likely to kill the parent as freezing temperatures. Tackle the latter by adding a thick mulch.

## plants at their best

- ❖ *Agapanthus*
- ❖ *Alcea*
- ❖ *Begonia*
- ❖ *Buddleja davidii*
- ❖ *Canna*
- ❖ *Cardiocrinum giganteum*
- ❖ *Crocosmia*
- ❖ *Cosmos*
- ❖ *Erigeron*
- ❖ *Eucomis autumnalis* 'White Dwarf'
- ❖ *Fuchsia*
- ❖ *Hebe*
- ❖ *Helenium*
- ❖ *Hibiscus syriacus*
- ❖ *Hydrangea*
- ❖ *Hypericum*
- ❖ *Lavandula*
- ❖ *Lavatera*
- ❖ *Lilium*
- ❖ *Lobelia*
- ❖ *Lonicera periclymenum*
- ❖ *Monarda longifolia*
- ❖ *Passiflora caerulea*
- ❖ *Perovskia atriplicifolia*
- ❖ *Romneya*
- ❖ *Rosa*
- ❖ *Solidago*

**above** Always label your cuttings. Keep the compost (soil mix) damp and pot up individually when well rooted. Protect them from frost.

## the greenhouse or conservatory

- ❖ Pot up pelargoniums and overwinter indoors. Reduce the height of each plant by at least half and it will soon send out new shoots
- ❖ Pot up *Scaevola* and overwinter on an indoor windowsill or in a frost-free greenhouse. Cut plants right back
- ❖ Pot up *Gazania* and *Osteospermum* and overwinter in a frost-free, dry place for planting out in the spring
- ❖ Plant bulbs for a spring display
- ❖ Plant biennial bedding plants in containers for a spring display (raised from the seed sown last spring)
- ❖ Plant hyacinths for early flowering under glass
- ❖ Check cinerarias for leaf miners (white 'tunnels' in the leaves). Remove the affected leaves or control with a systemic insecticide

**above** Fuchsias are really easy to root, and by taking cuttings now you will have young plants that can be overwintered. They will make good plants for next summer, or you can use them to provide more cuttings next spring.

**above** Take pelargonium cuttings now and overwinter the young plants in a light, frost-free place. Do not overwater, otherwise the cuttings will rot.

**above** This chrysanthemum is showing early signs of leaf miner damage. Often it may be possible to prevent spread if you act quickly and pinch off and destroy the first few affected leaves.

## the flower garden

- Deadhead plants regularly
- Feed plants in containers frequently
- Hoe beds and borders to keep down weeds
- Take semi-ripe cuttings
- Clip beech, holly, hornbeam and yew hedges, and most evergreen hedges, if not already done
- Plant colchicums to flower in the autumn
- Trim flower stems of perennial plants like *Dianthus* (carnations)
- Plant bulbs for autumn display
- Start planting spring-flowering bulbs
- Take fuchsia and pelargonium cuttings
- Start sowing hardy annuals to overwinter (only in mild areas or if you provide winter protection)
- Prune rambler roses
- Layer border carnations
- Mow the lawn except in very dry weather
- Water the lawn in dry spells, but a few good soaks will be better than many sprinklings that do not penetrate deeply
- Watch out for pests and diseases on roses and other vulnerable plants
- Feed and disbud dahlias as necessary
- Transplant polyanthus seedlings into their flowering positions in beds and borders

**above** Chrysanthemums and dahlias benefit from regular feeding. Use a quick-acting general fertilizer or a high-potash feed, but do not boost with too much nitrogen.

**left** Provided you can keep your greenhouse frost-free during the winter – ideally at a minimum of 7°C (45°F) – it is worth sowing plants to bloom next spring.

**above** Sunflowers and nasturtiums are a good colour combination.

**below** Old-fashioned garden pinks (*Dianthus*) form a lively border with buddleia in the rear.

# notes

Through trial and error, you can create the garden of your dreams, with the certain knowledge that you will have another chance to get it right the following year. Use these pages to record your planting successes and failures.

## annuals

Type ................................................................................ Sown ................................................................................

Variety ............................................................................ Thinned ...........................................................................

...................................................................................... Tip for next year ............................................................

Type ................................................................................ Sown ................................................................................

Variety ............................................................................ Thinned ...........................................................................

...................................................................................... Tip for next year ............................................................

## bulbs

Type ................................................................................ Planted ............................................................................

Variety ............................................................................ Flowered .........................................................................

...................................................................................... Tip for next year ............................................................

Type ................................................................................ Planted ............................................................................

Variety ............................................................................ Flowered .........................................................................

...................................................................................... Tip for next year ............................................................

## perennials

Type ................................................................................ Planted ............................................................................

Variety ............................................................................ Flowered .........................................................................

...................................................................................... Tip for next year ............................................................

Type ................................................................................ Planted ............................................................................

Variety ............................................................................ Flowered .........................................................................

...................................................................................... Tip for next year ............................................................

# climbers

| | |
|---|---|
| Type ......................................... | Pruned ......................................... |
| Variety ...................................... | Flowered ...................................... |
| ................................................ | Tip for next year ........................... |
| | |
| Type ......................................... | Pruned ......................................... |
| Variety ...................................... | Flowered ...................................... |
| ................................................ | Tip for next year ........................... |

# shrubs

| | |
|---|---|
| Type ......................................... | Pruned ......................................... |
| Variety ...................................... | Flowered ...................................... |
| ................................................ | Tip for next year ........................... |
| | |
| Type ......................................... | Pruned ......................................... |
| Variety ...................................... | Flowered ...................................... |
| ................................................ | Tip for next year ........................... |
| | |
| Type ......................................... | Pruned ......................................... |
| Variety ...................................... | Flowered ...................................... |
| ................................................ | Tip for next year ........................... |

# roses

| | |
|---|---|
| Type ......................................... | Pruned ......................................... |
| Variety ...................................... | Flowered ...................................... |
| ................................................ | Tip for next year ........................... |
| | |
| Type ......................................... | Pruned ......................................... |
| Variety ...................................... | Flowered ...................................... |
| ................................................ | Tip for next year ........................... |

**above** *Ipomoea lobata*, or morning glory, is a twining climbing plant.

**below** *Lavandula stoechas* subsp. *pedunculata* with purple sage.

# index

The publisher would like to thank the following people for us allowing to photograph their gardens: Dr Anthony Steven, Fardel Manor, Devon, (pages 44, 52) and Mrs. J. Smith, Edmonsham House, Edmonsham, Wimbourne, Dorset. Call 01725 517207 to confirm opening hours, (pages 38–9, 54–5).

**below** *Allium christophii* and *Salvia sylvestris* 'Lye End'.